DEFEND
&
AND
PROTECT

AIR FORCE

Robert Snedden

Gareth Stevens
PUBLISHING

Please visit our website, **www.garethstevens.com**.
For a free color catalog of all our high-quality books,
call toll free 1-800-542-2595 or fax 1-877-542-2596.

Cataloging-in-Publication Data

Snedden, Robert.
Air Force / by Robert Snedden.
p. cm. — (Defend and protect)
Includes index.
ISBN 978-1-4824-4106-2 (pbk.)
ISBN 978-1-4824-4107-9 (6-pack)
ISBN 978-1-4824-4108-6 (library binding)
1. United States. — Air Force — Juvenile literature.
I. Snedden, Robert. II. Title.
UG633.S64 2016
358.400973—d23

First Edition

Published in 2016 by
Gareth Stevens Publishing
111 East 14th Street, Suite 349
New York, NY 10003

© 2016 Gareth Stevens Publishing

Produced by Calcium
Editors: Sarah Eason and Jennifer Sanderson
Designers: Paul Myerscough and Simon Borrough
Picture research: Jennifer Sanderson

Picture credits: Department of Defense (DoD): 13, 24, 37t, Airman 1st Class Corey Hook 19b, Airman
1st Class Michael Dorus 20, Donna Miles 7, Master Sgt. Jeremiah Erickson 30–31, Master Sgt. Kevin
J. Gruenwald 29, Master Sgt. Scott Reed 3, 28, Mike Kaplan 11, Senior Airman Greg L. Davis 25, Staff
Sgt. Aaron Allmon 4, Staff Sgt. Bennie J. Davis III 32, Staff Sgt. Chad Thompson 42, Staff Sgt. Jacob N.
Bailey 8, Staff Sgt. Samuel Rogers 38, Staff Sgt. Tyrona Pearsall 23, Tech. Sgt. James E. Lotz 39, Tech.
Sgt. James L. Harper Jr. 36–37; Shutterstock: aarrows 5b, 7bl, 11b, 13b, 15t, 16b, 19t, 21b, 23l, 25b,
27b, 29b, 31b, 33b, 34b, 37b, 39b, 41b, 43b; US Air Force: Senior Airman Brett Clashman 1, 15b,
Senior Airman Brett Clashman 40–41, Senior Airman Kenny Holston 34–35, Staff Sgt. Kelly Goonan
10, Staff Sgt. Marleah Robertson 17, 45; US Air National Guard: Senior Airman Kari Giles 26; US Army:
Carlton Wallace 12, US Marine Corps: MCIPAC Combat Camera Lance Cpl. Hernan Vidana 6; Wikimedia
Commons: Airman 1st Class Nathan Clark 14, Alan Wilson 33, Bradley A. Lail 27, SRA LEE OSBERRY 43.

Printed in the United States of America

CPSIA compliance information: Batch #CW16GS: For further information contact
Gareth Stevens, New York, New York at 1-800-542-2595.

Contents

CHAPTER 1:
In the Air and on the Ground

When you think of the air force, some of the first things that come to mind may be pilots and their aircraft. Pilots are actually one of the smallest groups of people in the air force. They are supported by other members of aircrew and by a dedicated team of ground staff, who help the aircrew. Without the backup of engineers, mechanics, radar operators, and air traffic controllers, pilots would not be able to fly their missions safely, if at all.

An F-15 Strike Eagle releases flares designed to protect it from enemy missiles.

Defense in the Air

In many countries, the air force is responsible for deploying and operating ground-based air defenses, such as antiaircraft guns and air-to-air missiles. The air force may also operate early warning networks and defensive systems, guarding against ballistic missile attacks. Some nations, such as Russia, have an Aerospace Defense Force, which is a military organization separate from their air force.

The United States Air Force (USAF) is a massive organization and one of the world's largest fighting forces. It has more than 300,000 staff on active duty and nearly 200,000 civilian personnel. It operates nearly 6,000 military aircraft, including more than 2,000 fighter aircraft. The USAF is responsible for 450 intercontinental ballistic missiles and dozens of military satellites. The world's second-largest air force is the Russian Air Force, which can muster about 4,000 aircraft. About 750 of these are fighters.

ACT LIKE AN EMERGENCY MANAGEMENT SPECIALIST

Military aircraft fly from an air base. Every air force needs operational air bases. If disaster hits an air force base, whether in the form of an enemy attack or a natural disaster, it is the job of the emergency management specialist to get things up and running again as quickly as possible. Emergency management specialists work to keep their base operational whatever happens. They also run training exercises to keep base personnel ready for every eventuality.

The Role of the Air Force

The air force is one of the main branches of the military services. Its main mission is to conduct warfare from the air. The air force must protect its country from attack and it must be ready to attack the country's enemies.

The air force has many different responsibilities, including gaining control of the air (and so preventing attacks on its own country by enemy aircraft) and attacking enemy targets. It also supports ground troops (soldiers on the ground) by flying in supplies or providing covering fire. The air force may also be used to airlift supplies to disaster zones. The USAF's mission is to "fly, fight, and win in air, space, and cyberspace."

Vital supplies are flown in to help the victims of the 2015 earthquake in Nepal.

Beyond Earth

As well as flying aircraft, the USAF is responsible for operating the largest space program in the world. Crucial to the success of this mission are the efforts and skills of the Space Systems Operations (SSO) specialists. These highly trained personnel are responsible for everything from assisting in rocket launches to space-flight operations, tracking satellites, and detecting sea-launched ballistic missiles. SSO specialists have to think fast and decisively. They must keep a cool head and must be able to multitask under pressure.

CCATT at work

ACT LIKE AN AIR FORCE MEDIC

A Critical Care Air Transport Team, or CCATT, is a specialized medical team. The team works with a transport aircraft and its crew, to create an airborne intensive care unit, which can be used to fly critically sick or wounded patients to the hospital. After an earthquake hit Haiti in 2010, CCATTs worked to transport victims to hospitals in South Florida, where they could get the help they needed.

TAKE THE TEST!

Do you have what it takes to join the air force?

The air force is not just about aircraft—test your knowledge to see what you remember:

Q1. What is the USAF's mission?

Q2. How many military aircraft are flown by the USAF?

Q3. How many fighter aircraft fly with the Russian Air Force?

Q4. What is a CCATT?

Q5. Pilots make up the largest group in the air force. True or false?

Q6. If a natural disaster strikes an air force base, who is responsible for getting it up and running again?

Q7. Where did CCATT medics transport victims of the 2010 Haiti earthquake?

Q8. What do early warning networks guard against?

ANSWERS

Q8. Ballistic missile attacks
Q7. South Florida
Q6. Emergency management specialist
Q5. False
Q4. A Critical Care Air Transport Team
Q3. About 750 fighters
Q2. Nearly 6,000
Q1. "Fly, fight, and win in air, space, and cyberspace."

CHAPTER 2:
Air Crew

Pilots can be trained to fly combat jets, transportation aircraft, or helicopters. They may be called upon for many tasks. Some conduct air-to-air combat or ground attack missions, while others fly transportation aircraft to deliver support for ground troops or humanitarian aid. Helicopter pilots may take troops into combat or carry out search-and-rescue missions.

To become an enlisted airman, potential recruits must have a high school diploma and they must also pass a vocational aptitude test. This test measures whether or not a candidate has the mental skills for the air force. It also helps determine which air force career might be most suitable. All candidates are also screened for physical fitness.

A helicopter crew practice its search-and-rescue skills.

If accepted, candidates go on to basic training. This is an eight-week course to learn basic military skills. After this, they progress to technical training for their chosen career, such as engineering, electronics, transportation, or maintenance.

Officer Training

Officers are the leaders of the USAF. The first step to being accepted for officer training is to have a college degree. Officer applicants attend the Officer Training School. To guarantee trainees are capable of meeting the physical demands of the course, they have to pass the Air Force Physical Fitness Test during the first week of training. The two-month training program teaches land navigation skills, self-defense, and first aid. It also includes lessons in problem solving, team building, military customs and history, and terrorism.

• Fit and ready

THINK LIKE AN OFFICER

Officer training puts the pressures of leadership and command on trainees by having them demonstrate what they have learned with new recruits, and by leading their peers through various exercises. In order to advance, candidates will have to pass rigorous individual leadership evaluations at the Leadership Reaction Course.

Pilot Training

Recruits spend 10 months learning to fly a multiengined aircraft. They spend 18 months training to fly helicopters and 21 months training to fly combat jets. After this, when the pilots have their wings, they begin specialist training in the aircraft they will fly on operations.

Screening and Training

USAF officers begin flight training by passing Initial Flight Screening (IFS). This allows instructors to assess a candidate's ability and desire to learn aviation skills. Candidates must also pass a flight physical, showing they are fit to fly, and have a Student Pilot Certificate.

The initial flight training program consists of 25 hours of classroom instruction and 25 hours of hands-on flying for those who do not already hold a civilian pilot's license. The trainee pilots must be able to fly solo at least once before reaching the 17th hour of flight time on the course.

Trainee pilots practice escaping from a mock-up of a helicopter cockpit.

Training aircraft in formation

After introductory flight school, the trainees embark on a year-long course. They train for 10 to 12 hours a day, dividing their time between classroom instruction, simulator training, and actual flying. The officers learn navigation, aerobatics, formation flying, and how to rely on aircraft instruments. Depending on how the trainees perform, they will be assigned to an advanced training track and learn to fly a specific type of aircraft.

ACT LIKE A PILOT

Scrambling is getting aircraft in the air as quickly as possible to meet a threat. Pilots must be ready for action with little warning. For example, the North Atlantic Treaty Organization (NATO) forces aim for 10 minutes from detection of the threat to interception. In times of crisis, this may be shortened to as little as 2 minutes, but that requires pilots on standby in the cockpits of their aircraft.

Weapon Systems Officers

Weapon systems officers (WSOs) are vital members of the flight crew. They are responsible for cargo, management of troops, operating surveillance technology, and manning the aircraft's weapons.

In the USAF, WSOs are also known as combat systems officers (CSOs). CSOs are responsible for managing the mission, and in large aircraft, such as a bomber or transportation with multiple crew members, the CSO may also be the mission commander.

Being Challenged

To become CSOs, candidates must undergo a demanding nine-week course at Officer Training School. The course is set to challenge recruits both physically and mentally. CSOs are trained in weather forecasting, basic and advanced navigational skills, guidance and control systems, electronics, communications, and weapons systems.

Trainees spend time in a flight simulator to learn to fly a Globemaster transportation aircraft.

This training takes place in the classroom, in the simulator, and in various aircraft. After learning these skills, recruits will train to qualify as crew members aboard specific aircraft and mission types, such as search-and-rescue, helicopters, air-to-air refueling, bombers, electronic warfare, and long-range patrols. Some CSOs serve with special operations forces, helping carry out reconnaissance and attack missions behind enemy lines.

THINK LIKE A CSO

Air battles can move at speeds that seem almost unbelievable, so this means that CSOs have to think and act just as quickly and without hesitation. They are trained to bring an extraordinary level of focus and concentration to their task. CSOs are experts at using a wide range of high-tech equipment and weapons to ensure the safety of their fellow crew members, while successfully accomplishing their mission.

A CSO prepares for flight

TAKE THE TEST!

Do you have what it takes to join the USAF?

Trainees have to remember a lot of information to pass their tests. Check your knowledge with these questions:

Q1. What is another name for weapon systems officer?

Q2. What is scrambling?

Q3. You need a college degree to become an air force officer. True or false?

Q4. How long does helicopter pilot training take?

Q5. What does Initial Flight Screening do?

Q6. How long is spent training, each day, after introductory flight school?

Q7. Who is responsible for managing a mission—the pilot or the CSO?

Q8. What test is used to determine if recruits are fit enough for the USAF?

ANSWERS

08. The Air Force Physical Fitness Test
07. The CSO
06. 10 to 12 hours a day
05. It allows instructors to assess a candidate's ability
and desire to learn to fly
04. 18 months
03. True
02. Getting aircraft into the air as quickly as possible
01. Combat systems officer (CSO)

CHAPTER 3: Ground Support

Aircraft technicians specialize in the maintenance of an air force's aircraft. They ensure the high performance of the aircraft's engines and flying controls. Their job is also to maintain all mechanical, structural, and electrical parts of the aircraft.

An aircraft spends much more time on the ground than it does in the air. The ground equipment crew use this time to service the aircraft's electrical and mechanical systems, repairing and replacing anything that looks like it might cause a problem when in the air. They know it is far better to find a problem on the ground than in the air, so their work is done with great care and attention to detail.

Fixing Aircraft

Aerospace propulsion specialists must know everything about aircraft engines. They have to be able to find and fix any fault, including the fuel, oil, electrical, and engine airflow systems. They must remove and replace any faulty engine parts and perform tests on the repaired engine before reinstalling it in the aircraft. All this must be done as quickly as possible so the aircraft will be able to fly when needed. To be an aerospace propulsion specialist, candidates must pass their basic training. After this, they will do a course of up to 51 days in aviation maintenance technology.

THINK LIKE A MAINTENANCE SPECIALIST

The tactical aircraft maintenance specialist has to make sure that an aircraft is ready to fly at a moment's notice. The crew of the aircraft is completely dependent on the maintenance specialist for making sure that every system of the aircraft is maintained to the highest standards. The integrity of the plane and with it, the safety of the pilot and crew, come down to the skills and attention to detail of the maintenance specialists.

This technician is working to get a B1-B Lancer bomber ready for its mission.

Avionics Technicians

Avionics technicians maintain and repair the complicated electronics systems of modern aircraft. They start out as aircraft maintenance mechanics, and after two years, undergo specialist training to become responsible for the performance of the aircraft's avionics.

Avionics engineers need to work carefully to ensure every aspect of the avionics is working properly.

Aviation and Electronics

The word "avionics" comes from aviation and electronics. There are three aircraft systems that the avionics technicians are responsible for: communications and navigation, flight control systems, and electronic warfare. These systems work together to control the aircraft's radar, communications, and target-acquisition equipment. The avionics system is like the brain of the aircraft. If it fails, the aircraft cannot function and complete its mission. Avionics technicians have been described as the brain surgeons of some of the air force's most advanced and sophisticated aircraft.

The electronic warfare system protects the aircraft from any threats it encounters on its mission. It involves using jamming systems, which prevent enemy radar from locking on to the aircraft, and countermeasures to evade missiles. The system can also deceive enemy tracking systems to make them uncertain of how many aircraft there actually are. The electronic warfare system can allow the pilots of an aircraft to complete their mission without the enemy ever knowing the plane was there.

THINK LIKE AN AVIONICS TECHNICIAN

Avionics technicians learn to do things like replace radar antennae and to painstakingly troubleshoot the wiring of a computer system. Their instructors are all experts in their fields and cannot tolerate any carelessness. They know that a moment's inattention to detail could mean the loss of an aircraft and its crew.

TAKE THE TEST!

Could you work on the ground?

Take this test to see if you have the mental ability to work for the air force's ground crew:

Q1. Which aircraft system is used for jamming enemy radar?

Q2. Who is responsible for maintaining an aircraft's engines?

Q3. What two words does "avionics" come from?

Q4. The avionics technician is responsible for electronic warfare, communication and navigation systems, and _____?

Q5. Who makes sure that an aircraft is ready to fly?

Q6. What part of the human body is the avionics system compared to?

Q7. After basic training, how long is the course to be an aerospace propulsion specialist?

Q8. After how many years can an avionics technician begin specialist training?

ANSWERS

CHAPTER 4:
Into Action

Fighter pilots are the elite of the air force. Becoming a fighter pilot requires dedication—the selection and training process can take four years. Fighter pilots need to be able to think under enormous pressure. They also need to be physically very fit to deal with the stresses of high-speed air-to-air combat.

After completing their primary aircraft training, pilots have to choose one of four tracks to follow. These are the airlift/tanker track, the multiengine turboprop track, the helicopter track, or the fighter/bomber track. Pilots choosing to go down the fighter/bomber route begin a 24–28 week course of further training, during which they will log another 120 hours of flight time. Among other things, they will learn about low-level flying, flying in formation, and navigation skills.

Air force pilots fly dangerous missions. This pilot is flying a mission over Afghanistan.

Dogfighting

One of the main skills a fighter pilot has to learn is dog fighting. A dogfight is an aerial combat between fighter aircraft. It is really important that the pilot does not lose sight of their enemy. Fighter pilots say, "Lose sight, lose fight." The air force usually refers to a dogfight as air combat maneuvering. Pilots are trained to make full use of the electronic warfare system when they are under attack.

ACT LIKE A FIGHTER PILOT

Pilots have to be fit to fight. Fighter pilots accelerating and making tight turns can experience massive G-forces. The force of 1 G is the equivalent to the gravity a person feels standing on the ground. A force of 2 G would make the person feel twice as heavy as they do normally. Fighter pilots can regularly experience forces of 9 G. They need to have strong muscles and healthy hearts to cope with this.

Battle Managers

Even though they are often ground based, air battle managers have been described as "eyes in the skies." Battle managers can be weapons specialists who direct combat aircraft in hostile situations. They can also be surveillance specialists who gather enemy intelligence or search for enemy missiles and spy satellites. These officers provide the information needed to coordinate a battle, from directing dogfights to providing close air support for troops on the ground.

Battle managers must monitor enemy activities so they know where and when to strike.

Ready for Battle?

Training to be a battle manager is carried out over a nine-month course. Trainees are instructed in subjects such as the capabilities of friendly and enemy aircraft, when to take defensive and offensive measures, close air support, personnel recovery, the use of large force employment, and tactical control of high-performance aircraft. It is a tough course and the trainees have to meet a very high standard. Many trainee battle managers do not make the grade.

Battle managers have to be very familiar with the Joint Surveillance Target Attack Radar System, or JSTARS. This is an airborne battle management system used to monitor the activities of enemy forces across a wide area and pinpoint where an air attack may be needed. It is carried aboard a modified Boeing 707 airliner, equipped with radar, communications, and other systems, which can provide battle managers with the detailed information they need to make their decisions.

Mobile radar system

THINK LIKE A BATTLE MANAGER

Modern air warfare can take place at lightning speeds and every decision made could be crucial. The air force officers responsible for taking these decisions are the battle managers. They are even responsible for choosing the right aircraft for the mission. Their knowledge of strategy, and of aircraft and their capabilities, are vital to ensure a mission's success.

27

Combat Control

Combat controllers are part of the air force's special operations team and often work alongside elite forces, such as the Rangers and Special Air Service (SAS). The USAF combat control teams are usually first to go into enemy territory, scouting and preparing for other teams to attack. They operate in remote and hostile areas, helping pilots accomplish their missions by alerting them to the location of enemy forces on the ground. As well as being combat-ready, combat controllers are also trained in air traffic control.

Becoming a Controller

It takes around two years to train as a USAF combat controller. After an initial selection course, the Combat Control Operator Course teaches aircraft recognition and performance, air navigation aids, weather, radar procedures, air traffic rules, and other skills needed for air traffic control. All air force air traffic controllers will complete this 15-and-a-half-week course.

Trainee combat controllers then spend three weeks at the US Army Airborne School learning basic parachuting skills. This is followed by two and a half weeks studying survival techniques.

Combat controller

Combat School

After Airborne School, trainees spend 13 weeks at Combat Control School. There, they do physical training and learn small unit tactics, land navigation, communications, demolitions, and parachuting. On successfully completing this course, each graduate is awarded the coveted scarlet beret of the Combat Control Team.

Combat controllers must become experts in parachuting. Here, they are taking part in a parachute training exercise over Lake Mead in Nevada.

ACT LIKE A COMBAT CONTROLLER

Combat controllers require a formidable set of skills. They have to be able to perform precision parachute jumps into hostile enemy territory. Their navigational skills must be expert and they must be able to travel over any landscape in any weather conditions—they must be competent divers and skiers, too. Once in position, they will direct aircraft to hit enemy targets.

Combat Rescue

Air force combat rescue officers (CROs) are trained to carry out the rescue and recovery of injured servicemen from the frontlines. CROs organize recovery missions, train and equip rescue personnel, and manage and develop survival-skills programs. They are combat-ready as they may have to fight their way in and out of a difficult situation.

The CRO's mission is to rescue, recover, and return US personnel (and those from other nations fighting alongside them) from positions of danger, at war and in peacetime. All CROs are qualified in advanced weapons, free-fall parachute operations, combat dive and underwater search-and-recovery operations, rescue swimming, and rescues from confined spaces. They are trained to fast rope from helicopters to carry out rescue missions on both land and in the open ocean. CROs ensure that medical care gets to those who need it. They also provide supporting fire to keep enemy forces at bay while a rescue mission is carried out.

Pararescuemen practice rescue operations so that in an actual situation, they know exactly what to do to get personnel to safety.

Guardian Angel

CROs lead the Guardian Angel recovery teams, which include pararescuemen, who, as the name suggests, parachute in to rescue injured personnel. Guardian Angel teams also include Survival, Evasion, Resistance, and Escape (SERE) specialists. They provide command and control for the teams as they secure the rescue area, and are capable of mounting a rapid response in any environment.

• On alert

ACT LIKE A CRO

Since the US Combat Rescue special forces team was created in 2000, it has already carried out more than 12,000 combat rescue missions. As well as this, the team's skills and capabilities have been put to use in aiding the rescue of thousands of civilian victims of natural disasters around the world.

The Cutting Edge

Stealth aircraft are designed to avoid detection by enemy forces and are among the most cutting-edge planes flying in the world. The United States has led the way in stealth technology, but other countries, including Russia and China, are catching up.

Stealth pilots are selected from fighter and bomber crews. Even for highly experienced pilots, it usually takes a year to be accepted for stealth aircraft, such as the B-2 bomber. Trainee B-2 pilots first master the T-38 (a twin-seat jet trainer) to keep their skills and reactions sharp. They also have to complete an Initial Qualification Training (IQT) course, which covers basic skills in handling the B-2. Only three or four trainees take each class, which lasts six or seven months.

Guarding a B-2

The Blue Line

The Blue Line is an important part of stealth tactics. Carefully prepared for each mission, the Blue Line links the planned targets on a flight path, which is calculated to avoid the most dangerous enemy defenses. No matter how good their aircraft might be, the stealth pilots know that surviving a mission and ensuring its success, depends on thorough planning before takeoff. While en route to the combat zone, the stealth crew keep in touch with civilian air traffic controllers. This avoids the risk of collision with civilian aircraft, which would have trouble detecting the stealth plane.

Once it reaches the combat zone, the plane "stealths up" and becomes undetectable.

ACT LIKE A STEALTH PILOT

In 2013, two Iranian jets were threatening to destroy a US drone flying in international airspace. The pilot of an F-22 Raptor stealth fighter, flew his plane under the Iranian aircraft to check out the weapons they were carrying, without them even knowing that he was there. He then pulled up on their left wing and called to them, "You really ought to go home!" The Iranians fled.

TAKE THE TEST!

Are you ready for combat?

There is a lot to learn before takeoff. Find out how much you already know by taking this test:

Q1. What is the Blue Line?

Q2. How many weeks does a combat controller spend training at the Army Airborne School?

Q3. What does JSTARS stand for?

Q4. Name two things in which CROs are trained.

Q5. How many hours of flying time does a trainee pilot log on the fighter/bomber track?

Q6. What are the four tracks a trainee pilot can choose from?

Q7. Combat controller training takes more than two years. True or false?

Q8. How many combat rescue missions have US forces carried out since 2000?

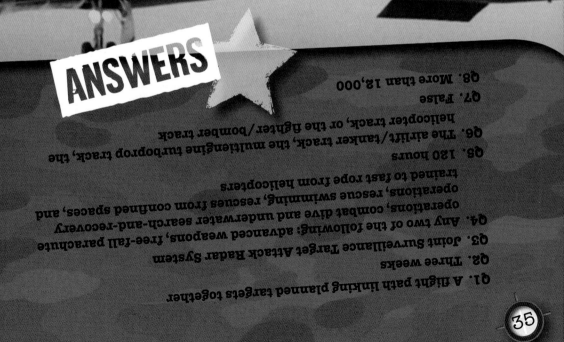

ANSWERS

Q8. More than 12,000

Q7. False

Q6. The airlift/tanker track, the multiengine turboprop track, the helicopter track, or the fighter/bomber track

Q5. 120 hours

Q4. Any two of the following: advanced weapons, free-fall parachute operations, combat dive and underwater search-and-recovery operations, rescue swimming, rescues from confined spaces, and trained to fast rope from helicopters

Q3. Joint Surveillance Target Attack Radar System

Q2. Three weeks

Q1. A flight path linking planned targets together

CHAPTER 5:
Transportation and Logistics

The job of the air force is not just to engage an enemy directly. Transportation aircraft carry out the important task of supplying the equipment and personnel needed to maintain combat aircraft operating away from their home base. They will also help transport ground troops and the materials they need to fight effectively.

Air transportation specialists make sure that food, water, medical supplies, and combat equipment are transported safely and quickly to troops on the ground. Part of their training includes the safe handling of hazardous, or dangerous, materials. It is their job to ensure that the cargo is loaded and secured safely.

The USAF are deployed to disaster areas. This airdrop of aid supplies took place after a hurricane hit Haiti in 2010.

Rapid Mobility

More than 120,000 air mobility airmen help the USAF deliver essential equipment and personnel for missions, from major combat engagements to humanitarian relief operations. USAF transportation aircraft depart for a mission every 90 seconds, 24 hours a day, 365 days a year. In 2012 alone, 38,000 airlift missions were flown, including 1,300 airdrops to coalition forces in Afghanistan. As well as moving cargo and equipment, the air force's rapid mobility capability gets medical teams to where they are needed, evacuating combat casualties, and saving lives.

Loading cargo

THINK LIKE A TRAFFIC MANAGER

The air force has billions of dollars worth of equipment, from state-of-the-art fighters to spanners. However, none of it is of use if it is not where it should be. Keeping track of everything, and ensuring it all gets to the right place at the right time, is the job of the men and women of traffic management. They make sure that aircrews around the world get what they need for their missions.

Air-to-Air Refueling

Air-to-air refueling is the process of transferring fuel from one aircraft (the tanker) to another (the receiver) while in flight. It allows aircraft to be deployed very quickly over large distances, to stay on patrol longer, and to fly farther into enemy territory, carrying larger weapon loads.

When aircraft refuel, the receiver aircraft approaches the tanker from behind to within about 100 feet (30.5 m). The two aircraft then match speeds. There are two main refueling techniques—probe-and-drogue and the flying boom.

Refueling

Probe-and-Drogue

Probe-and-drogue involves unspooling a hose from the tanker, at the end of which is a basket-shaped drogue. Once the hose has been fully extended, the receiver pilot extends a probe from the nose of the aircraft. The next step is to maneuver this into the drogue. This is not easy and the tanker will not start pumping until the probe is firmly sealed inside the drogue. Once refueling is complete, the tanker pilot disengages the drogue from the probe.

A boom operator aboard a Stratotanker prepares to refuel another aircraft.

ACT LIKE A BOOM OPERATOR

One crew member, known as the boom operator, controls the boom from his station at the rear of the plane. The boom is like a long tube that the boom operator has to steer carefully until it latches on to a part at the front of the receiver plane. Once this has been done, the tanker can start pumping in fuel.

TAKE THE TEST!

Are you ready for action?

How much do you know about air force logistics? Take this test to find out:

Q1. One method of air-to-air refueling is the boom method—what is the other one?

Q2. How many airlift missions did the USAF fly in 2012?

Q3. How close does a receiver aircraft come to a tanker?

Q4. Whose job is it to make sure cargo is loaded safely?

Q5. What does a traffic manager ensure?

Q6. How many air mobility airmen serve in the USAF?

ANSWERS

Q6. More than 130,000
Q5. That all the equipment needed for a mission is in the right place at the right time
Q4. Air transportation specialists
Q3. Within about 100 feet (30.5 m)
Q2. 38,000
Q1. Probe-and-drogue

CHAPTER 6:
The Ultimate Deterrent

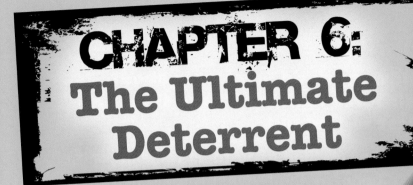

Loading weapons

The most formidable weapons managed by the USAF are its nuclear bombs and missiles. These are weapons of last resort.

The Air Force Nuclear Weapons Center (AFNWC) is responsible for managing the Minuteman weapon system. Minuteman is a land-based intercontinental ballistic missile (ICBM) capable of delivering three nuclear warheads over a distance of more than 8,000 miles (12,875 km). The AFNWC manages equipment spares, provides storage and transportation, and carries out repairs for the ICBM systems.

Missile Maintenance

Although no one wants to see it in use, the ICBM weapon system deters enemies. It is the job of the Missile and Space Facilities Maintenance specialists to see that the system is reliable and works. By inspecting, maintaining, and repairing everything from launch control systems to cooling systems, they make sure that the ICBM launch facilities are always operating at peak capability and are ready to go.

The systems on a Peacekeeper ICBM need to be thoroughly checked by a nuclear weapons specialist. One mistake could cost thousands of lives.

ACT LIKE A NUCLEAR WEAPONS SPECIALIST

It is the job of nuclear weapons specialists to inspect, test, maintain, and repair when necessary every part of the nuclear arsenal, from the warheads themselves to the bomb racks in the B-2 Stealth bombers. From ICBMs to gravity bombs and cruise missiles, the United States has a huge and diverse nuclear arsenal. Nuclear weapons specialists need to keep a cool head and work with extreme care and attention to detail, to ensure the reliability of these powerful weapons.

Have You Got What It Takes?

If you want to be a part of the USAF, follow these steps and you may reach your career goal:

School

A good education is important. You will need at least a high school diploma to enlist in the USAF. If you aim to serve as an officer or be a pilot, a college education is essential. A civilian pilot's license will also help if you want to train as a pilot.

An Active Mind

There will always be more to learn as aviation technology keeps improving. Be willing and ready to go farther than school lessons—read and learn for yourself and have an inquiring mind.

Personality

If you start a task, see it through to the best of your abilities. Others will be relying on you to do your job well.

Join a Team

Teamwork is vital in the armed forces. Even if you end up flying solo, you will still be relying on ground crew and others to do their job. Join a group, whether it is a sports team or a voluntary group, and develop your team skills.

Fitness

The first thing you will have to do if you join the air force is to get through basic training, so get fit and do not fail!

Glossary

airdrops dropping supplies or equipment by parachute

air traffic controllers ground-based controllers who direct the movements of aircraft

antiaircraft guns ground-based weapons that are used to try to shoot down an aircraft

coalition a temporary alliance

countermeasures action taken to deal with danger or a threat

drogue a funnel-shaped part on the end of the hose into which a probe is inserted by an aircraft being refueled in flight

drone an unmanned aircraft

early warning networks networks of devices that watch for an enemy attack

enlisted members of the army who are not officers

fast rope the technique of descending from a helicopter by climbing down a thick rope

intelligence information about an enemy, its plans, and its power

intercontinental ballistic missile (ICBM) a missile with a range of more than 3,400 miles (5,472 km)

North Atlantic Treaty Organization (NATO) a group of nations, including the United States and Germany, which came together for mutual defense

radar a system for detecting objects by sending out pulses of radio waves that are reflected off the object

reconnaissance observing an area to determine enemy activity

simulator a machine that provides a realistic imitation of an aircraft for training purposes

special operations forces highly trained units that carry out tasks beyond the means of regular service personnel

surveillance observation

target-acquisition the detection, identification, and location of a target, allowing it to be fired on if necessary

For More Information

Books

Bolt Simons, Lisa M. *US Air Force by the Numbers* (Military by the Numbers). North Mankato, MN: Capstone Press, 2014.

Miller, Adam. *US Air Force True Stories: Tales of Bravery* (Courage Under Fire). North Mankato, MN: Capstone Press, 2014.

Sutherland, Adam. *Armed Services* (On the Radar: Defend and Protect). Minneapolis, MN: Lerner Publishing Group, 2012.

Whiting, Jim. *Air Force Special Operations Command* (US Special Forces). Mankato, MN: Creative Paperbacks, 2015.

Websites

Find out about the history of the USAF at:
www.nationalmuseum.af.mil/education/kids

Read about the aircraft used by air forces around the world at:
www.combataircraft.com

See for yourself what basic training is all about at:
**www.airforce.com/joining-the-air-force/
　basic-military-training**

Index